Roger CPA Review

REG Flashcards

Regulation Key Terms and Definitions

ROGER
CPA Review

Acknowledgement:

This book includes contributions by members of the Roger CPA Review Editorial Team.

Copyright © 2019
By Roger Philipp CPA, CGMA
On behalf of Roger CPA Review
San Francisco, CA
USA

All rights reserved.
Reproduction or translation of any part of this work beyond that permitted by sections 107 and 108 of the United States Copyright Act without the permission of the copyright owner is unlawful.

Printed in English, in the United States of America.

Regulation Key Terms and Definitions

REG - TERM

Tax Filer

Unearned Income Medicare Contribution Tax (Surtax on Unearned Income)

Individual Taxation

ROGER CPA Review

REG - DEFINITION

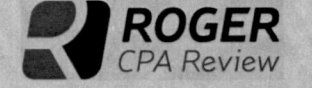

Someone required to file a tax return because their income is higher than their standard deduction, or someone who has net self-employment earnings of at least $400; is claimed as a dependent and has gross income over the standard deduction for a dependent; is receiving advanced Earned Income Credit (EIC) or Premium Tax Credit (PTC) payments; or is subject to the Kiddie Tax.

A 3.8% surtax charged on the lower of the net investment income or modified adjusted gross income (MAGI) in excess of $200,000 for most taxpayers, $250,000 for married couples filing joint returns, and $125,000 for married filing separate.

ROGER CPA Review

REG - TERM

Constructive Receipt | **"FOR" AGI Adjustments**

R11403 — Individual Taxation — R11904

ROGER CPA Review

REG - DEFINITION

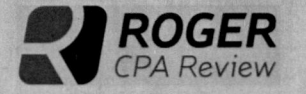

Term used to describe the date on which a cash basis taxpayer has income made available for use, which is the date on which it is considered received for tax purposes.

(*I EMBRACED Health & Farmers*) Adjustments added to or subtracted from gross income in computing AGI, including deductions for *I*nterest on student Loans, 50% self-*E*mployment tax, *M*oving expenses (military only), *B*usiness expenses (Sch. C), *R*ent/ royalty & Flow-through entities (Sch. E) (S corps, P/S, Trusts), *A*limony (pre-2019 divorces/separations), *C*ontributions to Retirement (IRA/ Keogh), *E*arly withdrawal penalty, jury *D*uty pay, *H*ealth savings accounts (HSA) and *F*arm income (Sch. F).

R11403   Individual Taxation   R11904

REG - TERM

Standard Deduction | Itemized Deductions

Individual Taxation

REG - DEFINITION

ROGER CPA Review

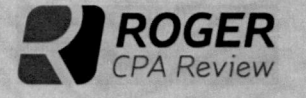

An amount a taxpayer may deduct from AGI in computing taxable income when deductions for certain personal expenses are not itemized, the amount of which depends on the taxpayer's filing status.

Expenses incurred by a taxpayer that may be deducted "FROM AGI" on *Schedule A*, instead of the standard deduction when computing taxable income. The deductions include (*COmMITT*): **C**haritable contributions, **O**ther **m**iscellaneous (e.g., gambling losses), **M**edical & dental expenses (10%), **I**nterest, **T**axes paid, **T**heft or casualty loss (from federally declared disasters or to the extent of personal casualty gains).

Individual Taxation

ROGER CPA Review

REG - TERM

Qualifying Widow(er) with Dependent Children Filing Status

Head of household (HOH) Filing Status

Individual Taxation

R11907 — R11908

ROGER CPA Review

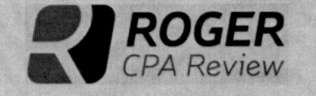

REG - DEFINITION

To qualify, taxpayer must meet the following criteria:

- Spouse died in prior 2 years and taxpayer qualified to file a joint return in year of death.
- Taxpayer provided over 50% of cost of maintaining principal residence of dependent child.
- Taxpayer must not be remarried as of end of year.

To qualify, taxpayer must:

- Be unmarried, and
- Maintain a home as the principal place of residence for over 50% of the year and provide more than 50% of costs of maintaining a household for a dependent:
  - ◊ "Qualifying Child"
  - ◊ "Qualifying Relative," including uncles/aunts, nephews/nieces, adult siblings or children, or certain step-relatives and in-laws. Dependent relatives further removed and unrelated persons do NOT qualify a taxpayer for HOH.
  - ◊ **Exception:** Dependent parents need not live with the taxpayer.

R11907   **Individual Taxation**   R11908

ROGER CPA Review

REG - TERM

Qualifying Child	Qualifying Relative

Individual Taxation

ROGER CPA Review

REG - DEFINITION

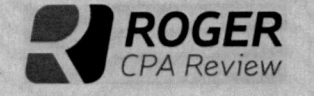

- No **J**oint Return w/ spouse, unless filing only to get a refund.
- **A**ge – Unless disabled, child must be:
  - Under age 19, or 24 if a full-time student for at least 5 months of the year, and
  - Younger than the taxpayer or spouse.
- **R**elationship – Taxpayer's child, stepchild, foster child, sibling, step sibling, half sibling, or a descendant of any such individual.
- **R**esidency – Child must live with the taxpayer more than half the year in the U.S.
- **S**upport – Child must NOT have provided more than 50% of their own support, not including scholarships.

A dependent **R**elative of the taxpayer, or someone who lived with the taxpayer for the *entire year*, provided certain qualifications are met:
1. Not a qualifying child of another taxpayer.
2. **C**itizen of U.S., or resident of the U.S., Canada, or Mexico.
3. **I**ncome for the year less than $4,150 for 2018.
4. The taxpayer provided more than half of the cost of **S**upport.
5. **J**oint return not being filed.

R11909   **Individual Taxation**   R11910

ROGER CPA Review

REG - TERM

Nonrefundable Tax Credits

Refundable Tax Credits

Individual Taxation

ROGER CPA Review

REG - DEFINITION

Tax credits that may be used to reduce taxes and, when in excess of the tax liability, may be carried back or forward, depending on the provisions of the credit, but may not reduce the tax liability below zero. Examples include:

- Dependent Care Credit
- Lifetime Learning credit
- Credit for Elderly or Disabled
- Family Tax Credit
- Foreign Tax Credit
- Retirement Savings Credit
- Adoption Credit

Tax credits that may be used to reduce taxes and, when in excess of the tax liability, may reduce the tax liability below zero, resulting in a refund to the taxpayer. Examples include:

- Earned Income Credit (EIC)
- Additional Child Tax Credit
- American Opportunity Credit (40%)

Individual Taxation

REG - TERM

Underpayment Penalty for Individuals

Alternative Minimum Tax (AMT) for Individuals

Individual Taxation

ROGER CPA Review

REG - DEFINITION

A penalty imposed on individual taxpayers who do not prepay a sufficient portion of their tax liability (through estimated payments or withholding) during the year, which results in a tax balance due of $1,000 or more. The penalty does not apply, however, if the taxpayer has paid in the lower of:

- 100% of the prior year's liability (110% for certain high-income individuals), or
- 90% of the current year's liability.

Taxes an individual taxpayer may be required to pay, in addition to the regular income tax, when taxable income includes certain items that qualify for preferential tax treatment, or when it has been reduced by certain deductions. It is the excess of the tentative minimum tax over the regular income tax.

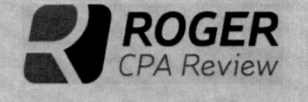

R11613   Individual Taxation   R11414

ROGER CPA Review

REG - TERM

Alternative Minimum Tax (AMT) Calculation for Individuals

Tentative Minimum Tax

Individual Taxation

ROGER CPA Review

REG - DEFINITION

AMT - Individuals

Regular taxable income
+/- **Adjustments &**
   Preferences (PLIERS)
= AMTI before exemption
− Exemption
   AMTI
× Tax rate (26%/28%)
= Tentative minimum tax
− Regular tax
= **AMT**

The minimum amount of tax that must be paid by a taxpayer based on multiplying the alternative minimum taxable income (AMTI) by 26% up to a certain amount, and 28% on the excess.

AMT Tax Preferences for Individuals

Individual Taxation

| **ROGER** CPA Review | **REG - DEFINITION** |

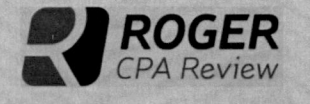

Additional items that are added to regular taxable income in computing AMTI due to their preferential tax treatment for regular tax purposes **(P)**:

- **_P_rivate activity bond interest** is fully taxable (private activity interest). Private activity bonds are used to finance nongovernmental activities, such as industrial development, student loans and low-income housing.

Individual Taxation

R11917

AMT Tax Adjustments for Individuals

Individual Taxation

ROGER CPA Review

REG - DEFINITION

Income or expense items computed differently for AMT vs. regular tax; therefore, they can increase or decrease AMTI for purposes of computing AMT. These include **(LIERS)**:

- **_L_ocal and state and income taxes**, all property taxes, and sales taxes paid are not deductible.
- **_I_ncentive stock options** are taxed when exercised for the difference between the exercise price and market price of the stock.
- **_E_xcess depreciation on personal property** over 150% declining balance when double-declining balance was used for regular tax purposes.
- **_R_efunds of local and state taxes paid** that were included in income for regular tax purposes should be taken out of income for AMT purposes.
- **_S_tandard deduction** may not be claimed.

Individual Taxation

R11918

REG - TERM

C Corporation

Section 351 Tax-Free Exchange

Corporate Tax

ROGER CPA Review

REG - DEFINITION

A tax-paying entity, taxed separately from its owners, created *formally* in accordance with the laws of the state in which it is considered domiciled, with shareholders as owners who have *limited liability*.

A provision that allows unincorporated entities to incorporate without significant tax ramifications by making exchanges of property or cash for equity nontaxable, provided only stock is received in exchange for the property and the party transferring the property and cash has control, consisting of at least 80% ownership when the exchange is complete. Services are excluded from the definition of property and are considered taxable exchanges.

R21601   **Corporate Tax**   R21402

REG - TERM

Accrual Basis

Dividends-Received Deduction (DRD)

Corporate Tax

ROGER CPA Review

REG - DEFINITION

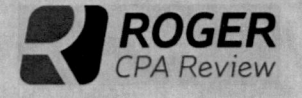

A method of accounting that requires a corporation to generally recognize revenues when earned, except for rents and interest received in advance, and expenses when incurred, provided they are paid within 2 ½ months of the corporation's year-end.

A corporate deduction equal to a percentage of dividends received based on the level of ownership:

- **50%** if a company owns less than 20% of the voting stock of another company (Unaffiliated co)
- **65%** if a company owns 20% or more, but less than 80% of the voting stock of another company
- **100%** if a company owns 80% or more of the voting stock of another company (Control)

Corporate Tax

REG - TERM

| Charitable Contributions | Adjusted Taxable Income (ATI) |

Corporate Tax

ROGER CPA Review

REG - DEFINITION

Donations made by a corporation to a charitable organization, deductible to the extent of 10% of adjusted taxable income (ATI), with any excess carried forward up to 5 years. Pledges may be accrued if paid within 3 ½ months of year-end.

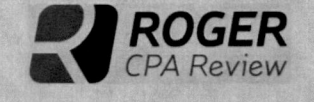

A corporation's taxable income before any deduction for charitable contributions, a dividends-received deduction, or any capital loss carrybacks.

R21805   **Corporate Tax**   R21906

ROGER CPA Review

REG - TERM

| Nondeductible Expenses | Accrual Differences |

Corporate Tax

R21407 — R21608

ROGER CPA Review

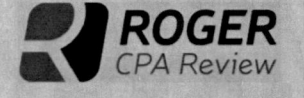

REG - DEFINITION

Expenses incurred by a corporation that are not considered ordinary and necessary for tax purposes and are, therefore, not deductible, including fines and penalties imposed by a government, costs of issuing stock, lobbying costs, compensation of executive officers in excess of $1,000,000 per year, and club dues.

Items that are reported differently by an accrual basis corporate taxpayer than they will be handled for financial reporting purposes, including bad debts, warranties, contingencies, unrealized gains and losses on marketable securities, and inventory losses.

Corporate Tax

REG - TERM

Accumulated Earnings Tax (AET)

Personal Holding Company (PHC)

Corporate Tax

ROGER CPA Review

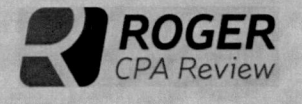

REG - DEFINITION

A 20% penalty tax is imposed on a corporation for accumulating excessive retained earnings to encourage the distribution of dividends. Excessive is considered to be $250,000 for a manufacturing company and $150,000 for a personal services company.

A tax on the undistributed income of a corporation that has 5 or fewer stockholders and earns 60% or more of its income from passive sources, such as interest, dividends, rents, and royalties. The tax on the undistributed amount is 20%.

Corporate Tax

REG - TERM

Schedule M-1 Reconciliation

Section 1244 Stock

Corporate Tax

ROGER CPA Review

REG - DEFINITION

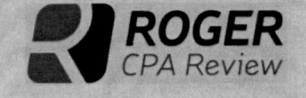

A corporation's reconciliation of book (financial statement) income (before special deductions – DRD & NOL Deduction) to taxable income. The reconciling items include both **Temporary** differences (bad debt expense, warranty expense, depreciation differences), and **Permanent** differences (municipal bond interest, 50% meals, fines, penalties, premiums paid on key person life insurance).

Stock acquired by a shareholder directly from a corporation with initial capital of $1,000,000 or less, losses on which are deductible as ordinary to the extent of $50,000 for a single taxpayer ($100,000 for married filing jointly) with the excess carried forward indefinitely and deductible as capital losses subject to the $3,000 per year limitation.

Corporate Tax

REG - TERM

S Corporation

Qualifications for S Corporation Status

S Corporations

ROGER CPA Review

REG - DEFINITION

A closely held corporation that, upon meeting certain qualifications, elects to be treated as a pass-through entity for tax purposes such that its income is not taxable to the corporation, but each shareholder is taxed on a proportionate share on a Schedule K-1.

In order for a corporation to elect S corporation status it must have (*Simple & Small*):

- Only one class of stock, with profits and losses allocated proportionately according to ownership (*Simple*).
- No more than 100 shareholders, with family members and their spouses being treated as a single shareholder, all of whom must be U.S. residents or citizens and natural persons—thus, entities, other certain trusts, estates, and tax-exempt corporations, may not be shareholders (*Small*).

S Corporations

ROGER CPA Review

REG - TERM

| Separately Stated Items | Passive Investment Income |

S Corporations

ROGER CPA Review

REG - DEFINITION

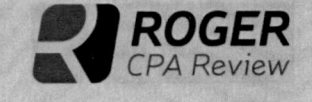

Items that are reported separately on the tax return of an S corporation (1120S) because of their tax treatments, enabling shareholders to each recognize their proportionate share of each item and handle it properly on their tax returns. They include capital gains and losses, Section 1231 gains and losses, dividends and interest, passive activities, charitable contributions, Section 179 depreciation elections, and tax credits.

Gross receipts derived from dividends, interest, royalties, rents, annuities and gains from sales of securities.

R31603   S Corporations   R31404

REG - TERM

Accumulated Adjustment Account (AAA)

Built-In Gains Tax

S Corporations

ROGER CPA Review

REG - DEFINITION

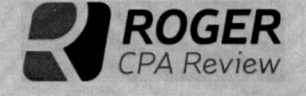

An account maintained to keep track of undistributed income and loss items for which the shareholders have already been taxed so that distributions can be distinguished between those that are taxable to shareholders and those that are distributions of income that have already been taxed. Amounts received out of AAA are not taxable when distributed.

A tax, calculated at the highest corporate tax rate, imposed on gains on disposals of assets that have appreciated prior to a tax-free conversion from a C corporation to S corporation status when those assets are sold within 5 years of the conversion.

S Corporations

Qualified Business Income Deduction

S Corporations

ROGER CPA Review

REG - DEFINITION

A **20%** from-AGI deduction for **qualified businesses** (i.e., certain non-service, flow-through entities, but includes engineering and architecture businesses) to help equalize the tax benefits received by corporations due to a reduced flat tax rate of 21% enacted by TCJA in 2017, calculated as 20% of **qualified business income** (QBI), subject to a Wage/Property Limitation, which is the greater of 50% of wages, or 25% of wages + 2.5% of unadjusted basis of qualified property.

- **QBI**—generally ordinary business income/deductions, but NOT compensation paid to owners for services, cap gain/losses, dividends, or interest income other than business interest income.
- **3 Taxable Income Categories:**
    - ◊ $0–$315,000 MFJ / $157,500—full deduction allowed for any type of business.
    - ◊ $315,001 MFJ / $157,501 up to $415,000 MFJ/$207,500—wage/property limitation will partially apply, and if a nonqualified business, another reduction applies.
    - ◊ Over $415,000 MFJ / $207,500—full wage/property limitation applies and must be a qualified business.

S Corporations

R31907

Partnership | Basis

Partnership Taxation

ROGER
CPA Review

REG - DEFINITION

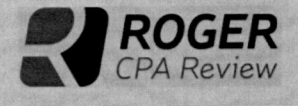

An arrangement, which may be formal or informal, in which two or more parties agree to operate a business as co-owners for profit. All partners have *unlimited liability*.

The amount the partner has "at risk" in the partnership, which initially consists of the cash or property contributed to the partnership, minus any liabilities assumed by the partnership, plus the partner's proportionate share of the liabilities assumed by the partnership, including those of the partner and other partners.

- *Increases* result from additional contributions of cash or property to the partnership and the partner's share of increases in partnership liabilities and taxable and nontaxable partnership income.
- *Decreases* result from distributions to the partner, assumption of any of the partner's liabilities by the partnership, and the partner's share of losses and nondeductible partnership expenses.

R41401   **Partnership Taxation**   R41702

REG - TERM

Outside Basis

Inside Basis

Partnership Taxation

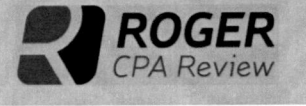

REG - DEFINITION

ROGER CPA Review

A *partner's* basis in the partnership.

The *partnership's* basis in partnership assets.

Partnership Taxation

REG - TERM

Guaranteed Payment

Contribution

Partnership Taxation

ROGER CPA Review

REG - DEFINITION

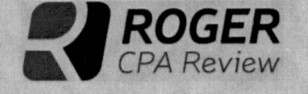

A payment to a partner that is not contingent on the partnership's profit or income, such as salary or interest, treated as if it were due to a third party but taxed as if a distribution of ordinary income. It is not considered a separately stated item to the partnership paying it, but it is a separately stated item to the partner receiving it.

Property that a partner gives the partnership for partnership use, which does not usually result in a gain or loss and with the partnership establishing a tax basis and holding period equal to that of the contributing partner (Carryover basis and Holding period).

Partnership Taxation

REG - TERM

Partnership Distributions

Limited Liability Partnership (LLP)

Partnership Taxation

ROGER CPA Review

REG - DEFINITION

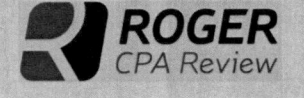

Withdrawals of cash or other property from the partnership that may be received by a partner as a distribution of current or prior period earnings (current distribution) or a distribution in partial or complete liquidation (liquidating distribution), reducing the partner's basis in the partnership, although not below zero, by the amount of money or the adjusted basis of property received.

A partnership in which some or all, depending on the jurisdiction, of the partners will have the same limited liability protection as stockholders in a corporation with the pass-through tax treatment of a partnership and the right of owners to participate in management of the partnership.

R41407

Partnership Taxation

R41408

REG - TERM

Trust

Distributable Net Income (DNI)

Estates, Trusts & Gift Taxes

ROGER CPA Review

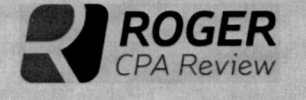

REG - DEFINITION

An artificial entity, created by a Trustor (Grantor or Settlor), who places property in the custody of one party, the trustee (control), for the benefit of another, the beneficiary.

The maximum portion of a distribution to the beneficiary of a trust or estate that can be taxed to the beneficiary, with the rest being treated as a tax-free distribution of principal.

R51401 **Estates, Trusts & Gift Taxes** R51402

REG - TERM

Alternate Valuation Date (AVD)

Income in Respect of Decedent (IRD)

Estates, Trusts & Gift Taxes

ROGER CPA Review

REG - DEFINITION

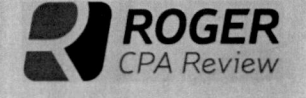

A date *six months* after a decedent's death that assets can be valued at, if they are not yet distributed and if electing the AVD, as opposed to valuing assets as of the date of death. The AVD can be used if it will reduce the value of the estate and the amount of estate tax due.

Collection of amounts earned by and due to the decedent as of the date of death, such as unpaid salary, that is treated as income to the estate and to the recipient (the beneficiary), who will declare it as IRD.

R51603

Estates, Trusts & Gift Taxes

R51404

REG - TERM

Allowable Deductions from Estate

Estate Tax

Estates, Trusts & Gift Taxes

REG - DEFINITION

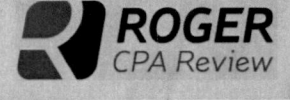

ROGER CPA Review

Amounts that reduce a decedent's gross estate consisting of state death taxes paid and claimed as a deduction; a marital deduction for assets transferred to a surviving spouse, charitable contributions authorized in the will of the decedent, funeral expenses, casualty and theft losses occurring during the administration of the estate, expenses of administering the estate, and liabilities of the estate.

The tax required to be paid by an estate (Form 706), calculated on the taxable estate and reduced for certain credits, including the foreign death tax credit and the unified credit.

Estates, Trusts & Gift Taxes

REG - TERM

Unified (Applicable) Credit

Lifetime Exclusion

Estates, Trusts & Gift Taxes

ROGER CPA Review

REG - DEFINITION

A credit equal to about 40% of the *lifetime exclusion* that has not otherwise been used, which is applied to reduce a decedent's estate tax.

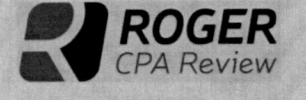

The amount ($11,180,000 in 2018) an individual can transfer during their lifetime or at death without being subject to gift, estate, and/or generation-skipping transfer taxes.

R51707

Estates, Trusts & Gift Taxes

R51908

REG - TERM

Gift Tax Return

Present Interest Gift

Estates, Trusts & Gift Taxes

ROGER
CPA Review

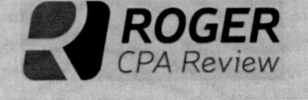

REG - DEFINITION

A tax return (Form 709) required to be filed by the giver, to report gifts given during the year in excess of the annual exclusion ($15,000 per individual; $30,000 if married filing jointly with gift-splitting election).

A gift that is immediately available to the gift beneficiary.

R51909   **Estates, Trusts & Gift Taxes**   R51610

REG - TERM

Future Interest Gift

Incomplete Gift

Estates, Trusts & Gift Taxes

ROGER CPA Review

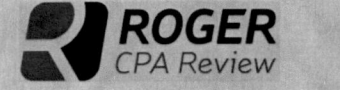

REG - DEFINITION

A gift that is not immediately available to the gift beneficiary and remains in the control of the donor for some period of time, such as the donation of a personal residence to a charity with title transferred upon the death of the donor.

A gift of a future interest that is *revocable* by the donor at any time until the property transfers. Essentially, no rights to the property have been transferred to the donee at all.

R51611   **Estates, Trusts & Gift Taxes**   R51612

REG - TERM

Portability

Generation-Skipping Transfer Tax

Estates, Trusts & Gift Taxes

ROGER CPA Review

REG - DEFINITION

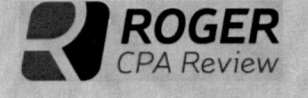

Allows for a surviving spouse to apply the decedent's unused lifetime exclusion in addition to the remainder of the surviving spouse's lifetime exclusion to future gifts and to the estate upon death.

A tax imposed when gifts are given to unrelated individuals more than 37 ½ years younger than the donor or related individuals who are more than one generation younger than the donor, such as grandchildren and great grandchildren, to prevent the avoidance of gift tax.

R51413   **Estates, Trusts & Gift Taxes**   R51614

REG - TERM

Modified Accelerated Cost Recovery System (MACRS)

Real Property

Depreciation

ROGER CPA Review

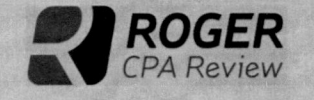

REG - DEFINITION

The depreciation method required to be used for tax purposes that allocates the cost of depreciable assets over a recovery period that is the same, regardless of whether the property is new or used, and is generally shorter than the useful life, ignoring salvage value and applying either the declining balance method with a switch to straight-line, or the straight-line method.

Land, which is not depreciated, and buildings, depreciated on a straight-line basis applying the mid-month convention.

R61401   Depreciation   R61602

ROGER CPA Review

REG - TERM

Depreciation

Mid-Month Convention	Tangible Personal Property
R61403	R61604

ROGER
CPA Review

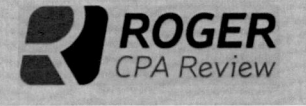

REG - DEFINITION

Real property is depreciated from the middle of the month in which it is placed into service until the middle of the month in which it is removed from service.

Assets, other than real property, depreciated using double-declining balance (DDB) with a switch to straight-line, except for municipal properties depreciated using 150% declining balance, generally applying the half-year convention but, in certain circumstances, applying the mid-quarter convention.

Depreciation

REG - TERM

Half-Year Convention | Mid-Quarter Convention

Depreciation

ROGER CPA Review

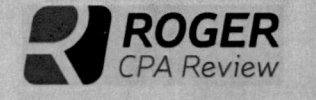

REG - DEFINITION

Generally applied to tangible personal property under which it is depreciated for ½ year in the year of acquisition and ½ year in the year of disposal.

Required when 40% or more of assets are acquired in the final 3 months of the year, depreciating assets from the middle of the quarter in which they are acquired until the middle of the quarter in which they are disposed of.

Depreciation

REG - TERM

Section 179 Deduction

Domestic Production Activities Deduction (DPAD)

Depreciation

ROGER CPA Review

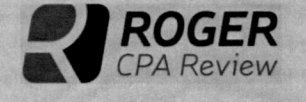

REG - DEFINITION

An election to immediately expense new and used depreciable business property, rather than capitalizing and depreciating it.

A special deduction under IRC Section 199, taken against income from production or production-related activities and designed to encourage domestic manufacturing.

R61607

Depreciation

R61708

REG - TERM

Ordinary Income Assets

Section 1231 Assets

Property & Special Property Tax Transactions

ROGER CPA Review

REG - DEFINITION

Assets, generally current, acquired with the intent of being used or sold in the trade or business, such as inventory and accounts receivable, which receive no special tax treatment, indicating that gains on disposal are fully taxable as ordinary income and losses are fully deductible and may result in a net operating loss (NOL).

Land and depreciable or amortizable assets (non-current business assets) that are used in the taxpayer's trade or business and **held longer than one year**, disposals of which result in either long-term capital gains (after depreciation is recaptured as ordinary income) or ordinary losses.

Property & Special Property Tax Transactions

REG - TERM

Long-Term Capital Gain

Short-Term Capital Gain

Property & Special Property Tax Transactions

REG - DEFINITION

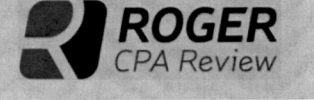

ROGER CPA Review

Gains realized on the disposal of assets that are held for longer than one year, qualifying individuals (not corporations) for reduced capital gain tax rates on such income.

Gains realized on the disposal of assets that are held for one year or less, which are taxed at ordinary income tax rates.

Property & Special Property Tax Transactions

REG - TERM

Section 1245 Property | Section 1250 Property

Property & Special Property Tax Transactions

ROGER CPA Review

REG - DEFINITION

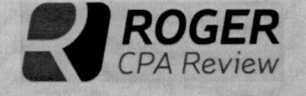

Depreciable *personal property* used in a trade or business. Section 1245 applies to gains on such personal property to recapture any depreciation allowed as ordinary income; the remainder is Section 1231 long-term capital gain.

Depreciable *real property*, such as buildings and structural components, used in a trade or business. Section 1250 recaptures gain on the sale of such property as ordinary income to the extent of "additional depreciation" taken on the property; the remaining gain to the extent of straight-line depreciation is "Unrecaptured §1250 gain" and is taxed at a maximum rate of 25% (special rate not applicable to corporations). Additional depreciation includes depreciation in excess of straight-line depreciation, or all depreciation if the property is held for 1 year or less.

R71605   **Property & Special Property Tax Transactions**   R71706

ROGER CPA Review

REG - TERM

Section 291 Depreciation Recapture

Uniform Capitalization Rules (UNICAP)

R71807 — Property & Special Property Tax Transactions — R71908

ROGER CPA Review

REG - DEFINITION

In addition to §1250 depreciation recapture on real property, 20% of the difference between the amount of depreciation recaptured under §1250 (i.e., "additional depreciation" to the extent of gain) and the greater amount that would have been recaptured if the asset had been a §1245 asset (i.e., all depreciation to the extent of gain) is also taxed as ordinary income to a corporation. Basically, the difference is the amount of unrecaptured §1250 gain that would have been reported if the entity was not a C corporation; 20% of this difference is also treated as ordinary gain. The rest is Section 1231 long-term capital gain.

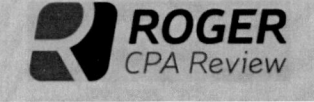

Requires companies with annual gross receipts of $25 million or more in previous 3 years to capitalize to inventory most direct costs as well as some of their indirect costs, such as storage, repackaging, and warehousing.

R71807 **Property & Special Property Tax Transactions** R71908

REG - TERM

Related Party Sales

Like-Kind Exchange (Section 1031)

Property & Special Property Tax Transactions

ROGER CPA Review

REG - DEFINITION

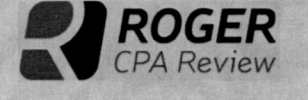

Sales between parties that are related by blood, marriage, or business relationship, such as partner and partnership or stockholder and corporation, for which gains are taxable but losses are not deductible and are added to the purchaser's basis.

An exchange of real property for similar property on which neither gains nor losses are recognized (unless boot is involved) and each party uses the basis of the property given up in the exchange as the basis of the property acquired.

Property & Special Property Tax Transactions

ROGER CPA Review

REG - TERM

Involuntary Conversion (Section 1033)

Installment Sale

Property & Special Property Tax Transactions

R71611 R71612

ROGER CPA Review

REG - DEFINITION

The sale of property being imposed on an entity, generally by a governmental agency, such as to permit the construction of a public works project, for which gains can be deferred and reduce the basis of replacement property provided the property is replaced within an established time period and all of the proceeds from the involuntary conversion are used in the acquisition.

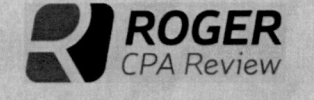

A special tax treatment that can be applied to the sale of assets by an accrual basis taxpayer allowing the gain to be taxed as the sales proceeds are received, rather than in the period of sale.

R71611   Property & Special Property Tax Transactions   R71612

REG - TERM

Exempt Organization

Public Charity

Tax-Exempt Organizations

ROGER CPA Review

REG - DEFINITION

An organization that is not subject to taxation after demonstrating it qualifies under Section 501(c) and receiving approval from the IRS.

An exempt organization that is a church, school, hospital, governmental unit, entity that undertakes testing for public safety, an organization that has broad financial support from the general public, or an organization that supports one or more organizations that are public charities, qualifying the entity for more favorable tax treatment.

R81601 **Tax-Exempt Organizations** R81402

REG - TERM

Unrelated Business Income (UBI)

Form 990

Tax-Exempt Organizations

ROGER CPA Review

REG - DEFINITION

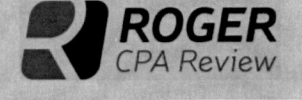

Income from operations of a business activity not associated with the exempt purpose of the organization, such as income from a church gift shop, which is taxable to a tax-exempt organization if it has more than $1,000 of UBI from all such business activities combined.

A form required to be filed with the IRS (and made available to the public) by tax-exempt organizations to demonstrate where they received their revenues from and how they were spent as a means of making certain that they continue to qualify for their tax-exempt status. Private foundations use Form 990-PF.

Tax-Exempt Organizations

R81903

R81604

ROGER CPA Review

REG - TERM

Corporate Underpayment

Individual Underpayment

R91601 — Penalties & Other Tax Issues — R91402

![ROGER CPA Review]

REG - DEFINITION

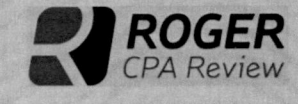

The insufficient payment of taxes by a corporation, considered to be the case unless one of 4 exceptions apply:

- The unpaid balance is *less than $500*.
- The *annualized method* was used and quarterly installments cover the tax on income to date, assuming it was proportionate to annual income.
- The *seasonal method* was used and quarterly installments cover the tax on income to date, assuming the relationship of the quarter's income to the current year's total income will be the same as the comparable prior year's quarter had to the prior year's total income.
- The amount prepaid is at least *100% of the prior year's tax liability*.
- .

The insufficient payment of taxes by an individual taxpayer, considered to be the case unless one of 4 exceptions apply:

- The unpaid balance is *$1,000 or less*.
- The amount prepaid is at least *100% of the prior year's* liability, or *110%* if the prior year's AGI exceeded $150,000.
- The *annualized method* was used and quarterly installments cover the tax on income to date, assuming it was proportionate to annual income.
- The amount prepaid is at least *90% of the current year's tax liability*.

R91601   **Penalties & Other Tax Issues**   R91402

REG - TERM

30-Day Letter

90-Day Letter

Penalties & Other Tax Issues

ROGER
CPA Review

REG - DEFINITION

A notification sent by the IRS to a taxpayer after an examination, assuming an agreement has not been reached, that specifies the agent's proposed tax adjustment and the reasons for it giving the taxpayer the option to do one of the following:

- Pay the proposed amount
- Contest the findings with the appeals division within 30 days
- Wait to receive a statutory notice of deficiency, a 90-day letter.

A statutory notice of deficiency giving the taxpayer 90 days to resolve the matter or file a petition with the United States Tax Court.

Penalties & Other Tax Issues

Sustainable Tax Position

Penalties & Other Tax Issues

ROGER CPA Review

REG - DEFINITION

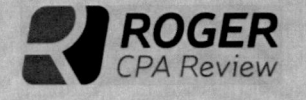

A tax position that is considered reasonably likely to be sustained upon examination, requiring various degrees of probability, depending on the basis on which it is being evaluated, ranging from the highest to lowest probability:

- *More likely than not* – a greater than 50% probability of being sustained
- *Substantial authority* – an approximate 40% probability of being sustained
- *Realistic possibility* – a 1/3 probability of being sustained
- *Reasonable basis* – a 20% probability of being sustained

Penalties & Other Tax Issues

ROGER CPA Review

REG - TERM

Uniform Division of Income for Tax Purposes Act (UDITPA)

Penalties & Other Tax Issues

R91406

ROGER CPA Review

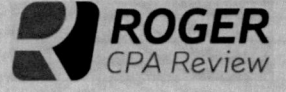

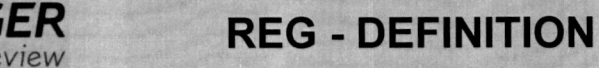

REG - DEFINITION

A federal law specifying how taxable income will be allocated among different jurisdictions when a taxable entity incurs tax liability in more than one jurisdiction, with different allocation methods for different types of income:

- *Rents* are allocated to the state in which the property is located and royalties to the state in which the asset generating the royalties is used.
- *Capital gains* are allocated to the state in which real estate and tangible personal property is located, and to the state of domicile in the case of gains on intangible personal property.
- *Interest and dividends* are allocated to the state where the taxpayer is domiciled.
- *Business income* is allocated on the basis of an average of 3 ratios, relating to the value of property owned and used in each jurisdiction, the compensation paid in each jurisdiction, and total sales in each jurisdiction.

Penalties & Other Tax Issues

ROGER CPA Review

REG - TERM

Controlled Foreign Corporation (CFC)

Participation Exemption

Penalties & Other Tax Issues

R91907 R91908

ROGER CPA Review

REG - DEFINITION

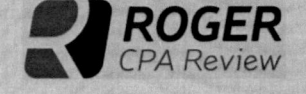

Foreign corporation where U.S. shareholders own more than 50% of the total voting power or value of all classes of the corporation's stock. A shareholder is considered a "U.S. shareholder" if they own 10% or more of total voting power of all classes of stock, or 10% or more of the total value of all classes of stock in the foreign corporation.

100% dividends received deduction (DRD) generally available for the foreign-source portion of dividends received from a "specified 10% owned foreign corporation" by domestic corporations that are at least 10% shareholders. of more than 365-day holding period required.

Penalties & Other Tax Issues

REG - TERM

Foreign-Derived Intangible Income (FDII)

Global Intangible Low-Taxed Income (GILTI)

Penalties & Other Tax Issues

ROGER CPA Review

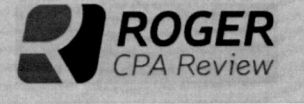

REG - DEFINITION

Intangible income (i.e., income from the ownership, sale, etc., of intangible assets) derived from serving foreign markets. For example, Disney receives FDII from licensing its characters to a European apparel company for printing on T-shirts to be sold in Europe.

A wide-ranging category of income designed to tax foreign income at a low rate immediately (rather than it being deferred).

Penalties & Other Tax Issues

Base Erosion and Anti-Abuse Tax (BEAT)

Penalties & Other Tax Issues

ROGER CPA Review

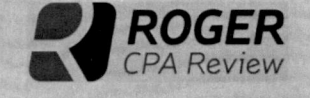

REG - DEFINITION

A minimum tax designed to protect against the incentive companies have to shift their profits to countries with lower tax rates (i.e., U.S. tax base erosion). An example of U.S. tax base erosion is the placement of high-value functions and assets in low-tax countries in order to generate profits offshore. Applicable to corporations with $500 million or more in average annual gross receipts over the previous 3 tax years.

Penalties & Other Tax Issues

REG - TERM

Breach of Contract

Negligence

Accountant Liability

ROGER CPA Review

REG - DEFINITION

Not fulfilling the terms of an engagement or agreement with a client, referred to as nonperformance, entitling the client, who is in privity, and any intended third-party beneficiaries, who are not in privity, to compensatory damages. Plaintiff must prove (*MILE*):

- *M*aterial misrepresentation or omission,
- *I*nfo caused harm,
- *L*ost money (damages), and
- *E*rror caused the injury (Breach or nonperformance).

Failure to exercise due professional care in the performance of an engagement, making the accountant liable to other parties to the contract having privity and various other parties, including intended third-party beneficiaries and possibly including foreseen and foreseeable third-party beneficiaries. Plaintiff must prove (*MILE*):

- *M*aterial misrepresentation or omission,
- *I*nfo caused harm,
- *L*ost money (damages), and
- *E*rror caused the injury (Lack of due diligence or Negligence).

R101601

Accountant Liability

R101602

REG - TERM

Privity

Fraud

Accountant Liability

ROGER CPA Review

REG - DEFINITION

Being a "party to the contract" and, as a result, being entitled to remedies in the form of compensatory damages for the nonperformance by other parties to the contract.

Ineffective performance with the intent to deceive, making the auditor liable to those with or without privity, including intended, foreseen, foreseeable, and unforeseeable third-party beneficiaries, which may be actual fraud or constructive fraud. Plaintiff must prove (*MILE*):

- *M*aterial misrepresentation or omission,
- *I*nfo *was Relied Upon*,
- *L*ost money (damages), and
- *E*rror caused the injury (Reckless or intentional misconduct – Actual or Constructive Fraud).

Accountant Liability

REG - TERM

Actual Fraud | Constructive Fraud

Accountant Liability

ROGER CPA Review

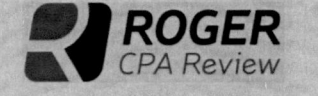

REG - DEFINITION

Making false statements with scienter or the knowledge of their falsity, such as expressing an unmodified opinion on financial statements that the auditor knows to be materially misstated.

Making false statements as a result of gross negligence or reckless disregard for the truth, not knowing if the statements are true or false, such as an auditor expressing an opinion in an audit report on financial statements of which an audit was not actually performed.

R101405   **Accountant Liability**   R101406

REG - TERM

| Scienter | Liability under the 1933 Act |

Accountant Liability

ROGER CPA Review

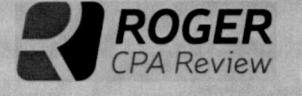

REG - DEFINITION

The intent to mislead, deceive, manipulate, or defraud with the accountant's knowledge of the falsity.

The ability of a plaintiff, with or without privity, to recover against an auditor under the Federal Securities Act of 1933 if the plaintiff can prove that the financial statements were *M*aterially misstated and that the plaintiff suffered a *L*oss, unless the auditor can prove that the audit was performed without negligence and the plaintiff was aware of the misstatement.

R101407   **Accountant Liability**   R101808

ROGER CPA Review

REG - TERM

Liability under the 1934 Act

Racketeer Influenced & Corrupt Organizations (RICO) Act

Accountant Liability

ROGER CPA Review

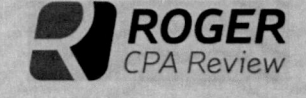

REG - DEFINITION

The ability of a plaintiff, with or without privity, to recover against an auditor under the Federal Securities Exchange Act of 1934 if the plaintiff can prove that the financial statements were *M*aterially misstated, which the auditor was actually or constructively aware of, and that the plaintiff relied upon the *I*nfo (i.e., financial statements) and suffered a *L*oss.

An act passed by Congress with the intent of punishing those engaged in racketeering by extending criminal liability to those ordering the commitment of racketeering or assisting in those involved in racketeering. Racketeering is an illegal activity carried out on behalf of an organization, such as the use of organized crime to commit illegal acts like extortion or the use of a legitimate business to perform illegal acts like money laundering.

R101809   **Accountant Liability**   R101410

REG - TERM

Tax Return Preparer

Internal Revenue Service (IRS)

Ethics, Professional & Legal Responsibilities

ROGER CPA Review

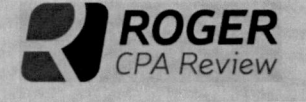

REG - DEFINITION

Anyone who prepares for compensation, or who employs one or more persons to prepare, all or a substantial portion of any tax return or claim for refund.

A bureau of the Department of the Treasury. The secretary is authorized by the Internal Revenue Code (IRC) to administer and enforce internal revenue laws.

Ethics, Professional & Legal Responsibilities

Treasury Department Circular 230

Ethics, Professional & Legal Responsibilities

ROGER CPA Review

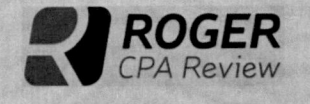

REG - DEFINITION

A set of U.S. Treasury regulations that govern practice before the IRS, divided into 5 sections:

- Authority to practice before the IRS
- Duties of and restrictions on those who practice before the IRS
- Sanctions for violations
- Rules for disciplinary proceedings
- Availability of public records

Ethics, Professional & Legal Responsibilities

REG - TERM

Securities Act of 1933 ("Truth in Securities Act")

Federal Securities Regulations

R121401

ROGER
CPA Review

REG - DEFINITION

An act passed by Congress requiring a company to register securities with the Securities & Exchange Commission (SEC) before they may be sold to the public by filing a registration statement, which includes a prospectus.

Federal Securities Regulations

Exempt Securities and Transactions under 1933 Federal Securities Act

ROGER CPA Review

REG - DEFINITION

Section 3 of the Securities Act of 1933 describes certain securities that are exempt, while Section 4 describes certain *transactions* that are exempt. **(ACID-BRAINS)**

- Regulation **A**– small offerings small public offerings (< $50M over 12 mo's; 20-day notice/waiting period; offering circular; can advertise/resell)
- **C**ommercial paper (notes, bonds) mature $\leq$ 9 mo's and used for Commercial (not investing) purposes. *Also:*
    - **C**asual sales by other than issuer, underwriter, dealer
    - **C**rowdfunding (< *$1M over 12* mo's *sold through online intermediary*)
- **I**ntrastate offerings
    - At least 80% of co sales are exclusive to state of incorporation and principal place of business, but buyers cannot resell outside the state for 9 mo's.
- Regulation **D** – Private placement offerings (Rule 504 < $5M, Rule 506 = unlimited)
- **B**rokerage transactions
- **R**egulated industries (Savings and loans – e.g., CDs)
- **A**gencies of the Gov. (Railroads, Municipal bonds)
- **I**nsurance contracts/Policies
    - Stock issued by insurance companies is not exempt.
- **N**ot for profit (charity/church)
- **S**tock dividends / **S**plits (i.e., exchanges with existing holders) as long as no commission is paid.

Federal Securities Regulations

R121802

… ROGER CPA Review

REG - TERM

Regulation D Summary – Private Placement (Rules 504, 506)

Federal Securities Regulations

R121803

ROGER CPA Review — REG - DEFINITION

Rule 504	Rule 506
Notify SEC within **15 days** of first sale (Form D)	
No general solicitation or advertising (generally)	General solicitation and advertising allowed if purchasers are all accredited investors
Resale generally restricted up to 1 year	Investment purpose only – Cannot resell for 1 year
Offerings ≤ $5,000,000	Unlimited dollar amount
Offerings must occur within a 12-month period	Unlimited amount of time for issuance
Unlimited number of investors	Unlimited *Accredited* Investors
	Nonaccredited ≤ 35 (0 if general solicitation)
Financial information given: Nothing	Accredited = Nothing Nonaccredited = Audited B/S and represented by sophisticated investor

Federal Securities Regulations

R121803

Securities Exchange Act of 1934

Federal Securities Regulations

ROGER CPA Review

REG - DEFINITION

An act passed by Congress that established the Securities and Exchange Commission, giving it powers to regulate the securities industry and establishing ongoing requirements for reports to be filed with the SEC, such as forms **10K** (annual audited report), **10Q** (quarterly reviewed report), **8K** (significant changes in the business), and **proxy** statements (items to be voted on at shareholder meeting).

- Registration and reporting requirements (S-1) under 1934 Act apply if either:
    - Securities are Listed or Traded on a **national exchange,** or
    - At least **$10 million in assets and 2,000 shareholders** (500 if unaccredited).

Federal Securities Regulations

R121704

Due Dates of 10K and 10Q Reports

Federal Securities Regulations

ROGER CPA Review — REG - DEFINITION

	Market Value of Out-standing Securities	10-K	10-Q
Large Accelerated Filer	≥ $700 million	60 days	40 days
Accelerated Filer	<$700 million, ≥ $75 million	75 days	40 days
Non-Accelerated Filer	< $75 million	90 days	45 days

Federal Securities Regulations

R121605

REG - TERM

Jumpstart Our Business Startups (JOBS) Act of 2012

Emerging Growth Companies (EGCs)

Federal Securities Regulations

ROGER CPA Review

REG - DEFINITION

An act intended to stimulate the economy by allowing emerging growth companies (EGCs) easier access to the public capital markets.

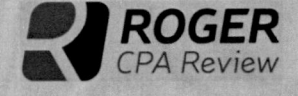

An entity that has less than $1 billion in revenues as of the end of its most recent fiscal year, entitling it to take advantage of the provisions of the JOBS Act, continuing as an EGC until the earliest of:

- The last day of the year of the 5th anniversary of the initial public offering.
- The last day of the year in which the entity achieves $1 billion or more in revenues.
- The date on which the entity has issued a cumulative total of $1 billion in nonconvertible debt over the preceding 3-year period.
- The date on which the entity becomes a large accelerated filer.
- When the company has more than 2,000 shareholders (500 if they are nonaccredited).

R121406   **Federal Securities Regulations**   R121807

Regulation Crowdfunding

Federal Securities Regulations

ROGER CPA Review

REG - DEFINITION

This exemption makes it possible for privately owned companies to sell securities to investors over the internet through an SEC-registered intermediary—i.e., either a broker-dealer or a "funding portal." Amounts are subject to inflation adjustments:
– Up to **$1 million** (as adjusted for inflation) may be raised in a 12-month period.
– Limits are set on amounts individual investors may invest per 12-month period (as adjusted for inflation):

- The greater of **$2,000 or 5% of annual income or net worth** (if less), for those with annual income or net worth less than $100,000.
- Up to **10% of annual income or net worth** (if less), up to a maximum of $100,000, if both annual income and net worth equal or exceed $100,000.

– Securities generally **cannot be resold for 1 year**.
– Disclosure requirements:

- Up to $100,000
  - Federal tax return
    F/S certified by principal executive officer
- $100,000 – $500,000
  - Reviewed F/S
- $500,000 – $1,000,000
  - Audited F/S —unless crowdfunding for first time, then Reviewed F/S.

R121808   **Federal Securities Regulations**

Regulation A

Federal Securities Regulations

ROGER CPA Review

REG - DEFINITION

Applies to offerings that raise **up to $50M** within **12 months**. Securities must be unrestricted equity securities, debt securities, and debt securities that are convertible into equity securities. The requirements are:
- SEC must be notified within **20 days** of the first sale.
- **Offering circular** (i.e., mini-registration statement) is required.
- Disclosure requirements:
    - Tier 1—Up to **$20M**, with up to $6M in offers by affiliates of the issuer.
        - **Unaudited** F/S
    - Tier 2—Up to **$50M**, with up to $15M in offers by affiliates of the issuer.
        - **Audited** F/S
        - Nonaccredited investors are limited to 10% of annual income or net worth, if greater.
- **Secondary sales are limited to 30% of the original offering** or any other offering in the first year.

R121809   **Federal Securities Regulations**

ROGER CPA Review

REG - TERM

Common Law Contract | **Termination of an Offer**

Contracts

ROGER CPA Review

REG - DEFINITION

An agreement between parties that may involve a promise for a promise (bilateral contract) or a promise for an act (unilateral contract) that, in order to be valid, must result from offer and acceptance with consideration and a lack of defenses. Common law deals with real estate and service type contracts.

The point at which an offer can no longer be accepted as a result of:

- *Expiration*—may be stated or will be after a reasonable period;
- *Revocation*—when offeror withdraws offer before acceptance;
- *Rejection* of offer by offeree;
- *Counteroffer* by offeree; or
- *Operation of law* as a result of the death or insanity of either party, destruction of the subject of the contract, or the illegality of the subject matter.

R131401   Contracts   R131602

ROGER CPA Review

REG - TERM

Contracts

| Early Acceptance (Mailbox) Rule | Acceptance Effective Upon Receipt |

REG - DEFINITION

ROGER CPA Review

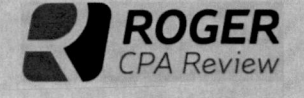

An offer is considered to be accepted when the acceptance is transmitted or dispatched (mailed) by the offeree, unless provisions of the offer or the means of acceptance make it effective only upon receipt by the offeror.

Circumstances under which acceptance of an offer is only effective when received by the offeror, such as when the offer specifies acceptance is only valid upon receipt, or requires receipt by a specific date; when acceptance is by an unauthorized means, such as acceptance by mail when the offer specified fax; or when an offeree submits both a rejection and an acceptance, in which case the one received first would be effective.

Contracts

ROGER CPA Review

REG - TERM

Consideration | **Voidable Contract**

Contracts

ROGER CPA Review

REG - DEFINITION

Something given or promised by one party to a contract in exchange for something given or promised by the counterparty that is *legally sufficient* to make a contract enforceable. It must be *of value*, which may include giving up a right, such as the right to file a lawsuit, but may not include past consideration or a pre-existing obligation, and must be *bargained for*.

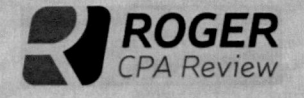

A contract that has the potential to become unenforceable against one or more parties due to certain defenses that may be asserted by the party wishing to avoid obligations under the contract, which may result from *duress, undue influence, misrepresentation of a material fact, mistake,* or *lack of capacity.*

Contracts

REG - TERM

Void Contract

Statute of Frauds

Contracts

![ROGER CPA Review]

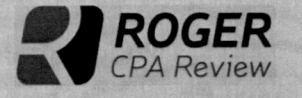

REG - DEFINITION

A contract that is invalid and unenforceable from the onset due to *extreme duress*, *fraud in the execution*, *illegal subject matter*, or the fact that a party has been adjudicated as *insane*.

A provision requiring certain contracts to be in writing in order for them to be enforceable because they are more susceptible to fraud, including contracts for (*GROSS*): the sale of **G**oods for $500 or more, sales of **R**eal estate, bilateral contracts that cannot be completed within **O**ne year, contracts involving **S**uretyship where one party guarantees the indebtedness of another, and **S**tatements made in consideration of marriage.

R131407   Contracts   R131708

ROGER CPA Review

REG - TERM

Uniform Commercial Code (UCC)

Firm Offer

R141401 — Sales Contracts — R141402

ROGER CPA Review

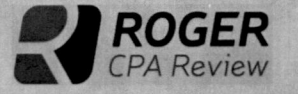

REG - DEFINITION

A set of laws that regulate commerce within the U.S. and establish guidelines related to the sale of personal property (UCC Article 2) but do not govern sales of real property or the providing of services.

An offer that cannot be revoked, despite a lack of consideration from the offeree, provided it is from a merchant, is signed, and expires after a specified period of time, not to exceed 3 months.

R141401

Sales Contracts

R141402

ROGER CPA Review

REG - TERM

| Implied Warranty of Title & Infringement | Implied Warranty of Merchantability |

R141403 — Sales Contracts — R141404

ROGER CPA Review

REG - DEFINITION

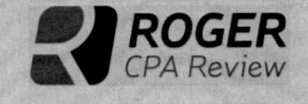

An automatic warranty associated with the sale of goods in which the seller warrants *good title*, that the transfer is rightful and legal, there are no liens or encumbrances on the property, and the transfer does not violate the rights of third parties, which may only be disclaimed with an explicit statement disclaiming the warranty in the sales contract.

An automatic warranty associated with the sale of goods in which the seller warrants that the goods are in fair condition (average, fair quality) for their ordinary purpose and conform to claims on the product's packaging, which may be disclaimed by phrases such as "as is" or "with all faults" in the sales contract.

Sales Contracts

REG - TERM

Implied Warranty of Fitness for a Particular Purpose

Express Warranty

Sales Contracts

ROGER CPA Review

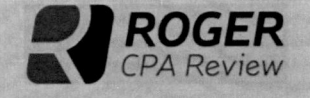

REG - DEFINITION

A warranty associated with the sale of goods when the buyer is relying on the seller's judgment that the goods will be useful for the buyer's specific needs, which may be disclaimed in writing with a phrase such as "as is" or "with all faults."

A statement or claim made by the seller that becomes a basis of the transaction and may not be disclaimed.

R141405

Sales Contracts

R141406

REG - TERM

Product Liability

Sales Contracts

ROGER CPA Review

REG - DEFINITION

A manufacturer's or seller's liability to compensate buyers if the product causes injury or illness, which may be asserted on the basis of any of the following:

- **Breach of warranty**—Buyer suffers injury and can demonstrate that the injury resulted from the breach of an express or implied warranty that was not properly disclaimed.
- **Negligence**—A party's careless actions cause harm to the other party requiring the plaintiff to prove an absence of due care, a defect in the product that was caused by carelessness, and damages to the plaintiff that resulted from the defect.
- **Strict liability**—Makes the defendant liable, even in circumstances where the plaintiff did not apply care in the use of the product and was not in privity of contract with the defendant, requiring only that the plaintiff prove that an injury was suffered, that the seller was in the business of selling the product, and that the product was sold in an unreasonably dangerous condition due to the defect.

Sales Contracts

R141607

REG - TERM

Seller Remedies

Buyer Remedies

Sales Contracts

ROGER CPA Review

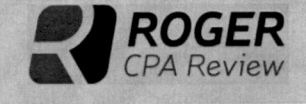

REG - DEFINITION

Recourse available to a seller when a buyer is in breach of a sales contract, which may include the right to *resell the goods*, the right to *stop* the common carrier from delivering the goods, the right to *cancel* the contract, and the right to *recover* incidental and consequential, but not punitive, damages.

Recourse available to a buyer when a seller is in breach of a sales contract, which may include *accepting some, all, or none* of the goods; *cover*, which is the purchase of substitute goods and recovering any additional cost from the seller; *specific performance* in the case of goods that are unique; *incidental and consequential*, but not punitive, damages; and the right to *rescind* the contract.

Sales Contracts

ROGER CPA Review

REG - TERM

General Partnership

Partner Rights

Business Structures

ROGER CPA Review

REG - DEFINITION

An association between two or more parties to operate a business as co-owners for a profit. It is *informally* created since all partners have *unlimited liability* for contracts and debts. It is not taxed as a separate entity but instead, treated as a *pass-through* entity with its owners responsible for taxes on its taxable activities.

Three basic rights of a partner, which include:

- The right to an equal share of *profits,* referred to as the partnership *interest (fully transferable)*;
- The right to *use partnership property* for partnership purposes; and
- The right to *participate in the management* of the business (voting, contracts, and debts).

R151401 **Business Structures** R151602

ROGER CPA Review

REG - TERM

Actual Authority | **Apparent (Ostensible) Authority**

Business Structures

ROGER CPA Review

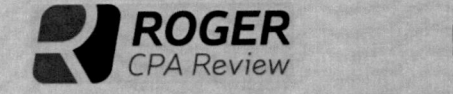

REG - DEFINITION

The ability to bind the partnership and the partners, which may be expressed when the partnership has *explicitly stated* that the partner has the authority, or *implied* when the partner's duties and responsibilities cannot be fulfilled otherwise.

The ability to bind the partnership and the partners without the actual authority to do so but as a result of a third party in *good faith* reasonably assuming that the partner has the authority based on actions of the partnership and the other partners.

Business Structures

ROGER CPA Review

REG - TERM

Notice | **Limited Partnership**

Business Structures

R151405 — R151406

ROGER CPA Review

REG - DEFINITION

The notification of third parties that a partner does not have the authority to bind the partnership and the other partners beginning when the notice is given, which might be *actual*, in which case the third parties are told directly, generally required when the third party has done business with the partnership before, or *constructive*, in which case notice is published in a manner that third parties should reasonably be expected to be aware of, such as in trade periodicals, which is considered sufficient for parties that have not previously done business with the partnership.

A partnership (governed by RULPA - Revised Uniform Limited Partnership Act) with one or more general partners and one or more limited partners. A general partner has *unlimited liability* for the obligations of the partnership. A limited partner's liability for obligations is *limited* to the amount invested in the partnership.

Business Structures

REG - TERM

C Corporation | S Corporation

Business Structures

ROGER CPA Review

REG - DEFINITION

An entity separate from its owners, governed by the laws established under the Model Business Corporation Act (MBCA) and providing its owners with *limited liability*. It is a *taxable entity* (1120), with an independent life (perpetuity) and a centralized management (board of directors).

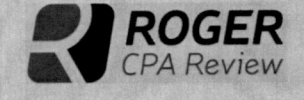

A corporation that provides its owners the same liability-related benefits as a C Corporation (limited liability), but it is not taxed as a separate entity but instead, treated as a *pass-through* entity with its owners responsible for taxes on its taxable activities. Must be *small* (no more than 100 shareholders) and *simple* with only one class of stock.

Business Structures

ROGER CPA Review

REG - TERM

Board of Directors

Business Structures

R151609

ROGER CPA Review

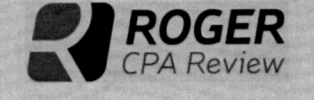

REG - DEFINITION

The board of directors are in charge of the *general operations* of the corporation. Some of the important principles associated with the board are:

- They must act as a board (act as a group).
- They are Not considered *agents*.
- Adopt the *Bylaws* (rules and regulations that help to guide the internal management).
- Reacquire *treasury stock* (TS), unless insolvent or makes them insolvent (TS is stock that is authorized, issued, but Not outstanding).
- Declare dividends.
- The Board Selects the **officers** (e.g., president) who:
  - Are in charge of *day-to-day* operations
  - Are considered Agents of the Corporation
  - Have the right to be Indemnified (right to reimbursement)

Business Structures

Shareholders' Rights

Business Structures

ROGER CPA Review

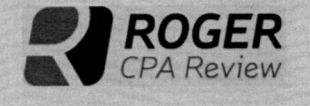

REG - DEFINITION

The shareholders of a corporation have various rights.

- Right to **vote** for the following:
    1) Board of Directors
    2) Liquidating Dividends
    3) Dissolve Corporation
    4) Mergers/Consolidations
    5) Amend the Articles of Incorporation
    6) Loans to Directors
- They are Not considered an *Agent*.
- *Transfer shares* without approval (freely transferable).
- Right to declared dividends (unsecured creditor).
- Right to inspect books and records (*Inspection Rights*).
- *Appraisal Right* – Right to get stock appraised if disagree with merger.
- Right to bring a *derivative lawsuit* → sue in name of corporation.
- *Preemptive right* – prevent dilution of ownership with newly authorized stock only.
- Limited liability unless *pierce the corporate veil* (if fraudulent corporation, commingled funds, undercapitalized).

Business Structures

R151610

ROGER CPA Review

REG - TERM

Workers' Compensation Laws | **Federal Unemployment Tax Act (FUTA)**

Regulation of Business Employment, Environment & Antitrust

ROGER CPA Review

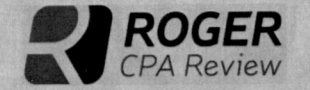

REG - DEFINITION

Laws guaranteeing payment to an injured or ill employee for job-related injuries or illness, regardless of fault, and barring the employee from suing the employer for negligence.

A tax paid by the employer (calculated as a percentage of wages paid) to have benefits available for employees who are terminated unless they left employment voluntarily (quit), refused to accept equivalent work available, or were dismissed for illegal activity.

R161401 **Regulation of Business Employment, Environment & Antitrust** R161602

REG - TERM

Federal Insurance Contributions Act (FICA)

Employment Retirement Income Security Act (ERISA)

Regulation of Business Employment, Environment & Antitrust

ROGER CPA Review

REG - DEFINITION

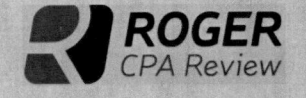

A tax paid by both employer and employee used to pay Social Security benefits in the form of old age retirement benefits, benefits to survivors and divorced spouses, payments for disability and to disabled children, and Medicare benefits.

A law applicable to employers who provide private pension benefits to employees, requiring that plans cover all employees falling within similar classes, that amounts paid by employees vest immediately and amounts paid by the employer vest within a reasonable time, and that the employer make contributions to a trustee on a timely basis.

R161403 **Regulation of Business Employment, Environment & Antitrust** R161604

ROGER CPA Review

REG - TERM

| Real Property | Personal Property |

Property Law & Intellectual Property Rights

R171401   R171602

ROGER CPA Review

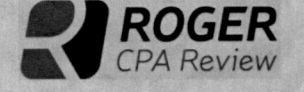

REG - DEFINITION

Land and permanent attachments to land such as buildings.

All property other than real property, including tangible personal property which has physical substance, such as furniture and equipment, and intangible personal property often representing contractual or legal rights, such as patents and copyrights.

Property Law & Intellectual Property Rights

ROGER CPA Review

REG - TERM

Fixture

Types of Deeds

Property Law & Intellectual Property Rights

ROGER CPA Review

REG - DEFINITION

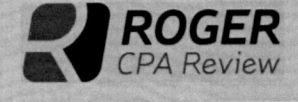

Personal property attached (affixed) to real property that may be classified as real or personal property depending on how it is attached, how it is used, and the intention of the parties.

A Deed is a document of title identifying real property and its owners that is used to transfer rights to property. Types of deeds include:

- **Quitclaim Deed ("As-is")**—a document in which the signer is relinquishing any rights they may have in a property without providing any assurance as to what rights, if any, they do have.

- **Grant Deed (Bargain and Sale Deed or Special Warranty Deed)**—guarantees a transferee that the property was not encumbered during the time it was held by the transferor.

- **Warranty Deed (General Warranty Deed)**—guarantees a transferee that there are no encumbrances that would interfere with the ability of the transferee to take good title to the property covered.

Property Law & Intellectual Property Rights

ROGER CPA Review

REG - TERM

Interest in Real Property | **Concurrent Ownership**

R171405 — Property Law & Intellectual Property Rights — R171606

ROGER CPA Review

REG - DEFINITION

A claim to real property that may be *fee simple*, which is outright ownership; *fee simple defeasible*, which is outright ownership upon the achievement of a condition or the occurrence of an event; *life interest,* which is a claim to the property for the lifetime of the holder or some other party; or a *leasehold interest*, which gives a lessee rights to the property during the term of the lease.

When two or more parties have rights to the same property simultaneously, which may be in the form of *tenancy in common* (ownership rights in the same property, in any proportion, without a right of survivorship), *joint tenancy* (ownership rights in the same property, that are equal in all respects, with the right of survivorship, but with each joint tenant having the ability to transfer their interest prior to death, without any right of survivorship), or *tenancy by the entirety* (when two parties, such as spouses, own property jointly giving each spouse a right of survivorship, which is severed upon divorce, death, or mutual agreement).

R171405   **Property Law & Intellectual Property Rights**   R171606

REG - TERM

Mortgage

Money Laundering Control Act

Property Law & Intellectual Property Rights

ROGER CPA Review

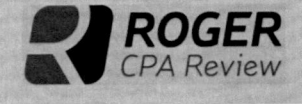

REG - DEFINITION

A security interest in real property, which the buyer may **Assume**: The buyer of real property accepts liability for the unpaid balance of a mortgage secured by the property, but the seller remains liable as well. The property may also be taken **Subject To**: The buyer of real property makes payments on the mortgage debt, but does not accept liability for it and the seller remains liable.

Makes money laundering, which is making money gained through illegitimate means appear as if it was earned legally, a federal crime.

R171407   **Property Law & Intellectual Property Rights**   R171608

ROGER CPA Review

REG - TERM

| Agency | Fully Disclosed Principal |

Agency

ROGER CPA Review

REG - DEFINITION

A relationship in which one party, an agent, represents the interests of, and is authorized to obligate, another party, the principal. The agent has a *fiduciary duty* to be loyal to the principal in an agency relationship and to look out for the principal's best interests in all matters where the agent is acting on behalf of the principal.

An arrangement under which third parties dealing with an agent know both that they are dealing with an agent on behalf of a principal as well as the identity of the principal, as a result of which, the third party may hold the principal liable for all authorized actions of the agent, but may not hold the agent liable.

R181701   Agency   R181702

ROGER CPA Review

REG - TERM

Partially Disclosed Principal | **Undisclosed Principal**

Agency

ROGER CPA Review

REG - DEFINITION

An arrangement under which third parties dealing with an agent are aware that they are dealing with an agent on behalf of the principal but are not aware of the principal's identity, as a result of which, the third party may hold the agent liable, or may hold the principal liable if they become aware of the principal's identity, giving the agent recourse against the principal for any losses resulting from authorized actions.

An arrangement under which third parties dealing with an agent are unaware of the fact that they are dealing with an agent and are operating under the assumption that the agent is acting in the capacity of a principal, as a result of which, the agent is liable to the third party but has recourse against the principal for any losses resulting from authorized actions.

Agency

ROGER CPA Review — REG - TERM

Secured Transactions

Collateral

Purchase Money Security Interest (PMSI)

ROGER CPA Review

REG - DEFINITION

A debtor's property, which may also include proceeds or after-acquired property that is pledged to a creditor as security for a debt, increasing the likelihood that the debtor will satisfy the obligation in order to retrieve the collateral, and giving the creditor an alternative source of obtaining value in the case that the debtor does not satisfy the obligation. Types of collateral include Inventory, equipment, consumer goods and chattel paper.

A security interest in collateral that is generally of a *higher priority* than all other security interests in the same collateral (*DOTS*) including the **D**ebtor, which requires attachment; as well as **O**ther creditors with interest in the collateral, a **T**rustee in bankruptcy, and **S**ubsequent purchasers of the collateral from the debtor not having knowledge of the security interest, each of which require attachment and perfection.

Secured Transactions

REG - TERM

Secured Transactions

Attachment

Perfection

ROGER CPA Review

REG - DEFINITION

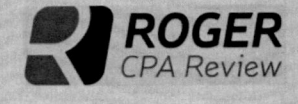

The obtaining of a security interest in collateral by a creditor which occurs upon the occurrence of the last of the following 3 conditions (*PIG*):

- Debtor obtaining *rights* to the property (*P*roperty owned by debtor);
- The creditor obtaining an *I*nterest in the property (either through possession or obtaining a signed security agreement); and
- The creditor *G*iving value to the debtor (which may not be a promise to give value in the future, but may be the extension of credit, such as approving a line of credit).

A process (which cannot be effective before attachment) that can occur in any of the following 3 ways (*FAT*):

- *F*iling of a financing statement,
- *A*utomatic perfection of a PMSI, or
- *T*aking possession of the collateral, any of which gives a creditor legally enforceable rights to collateral against the debtor and others with security interests in the collateral, who do not have a perfected interest or who perfected their security interest later.

Secured Transactions

REG - TERM

Financing Statement

Automatic Perfection of a PMSI

Secured Transactions

ROGER CPA Review

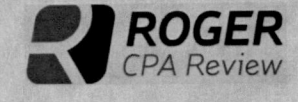

REG - DEFINITION

A document filed with an appropriate public office that describes the collateral, gives the name and address of the creditor, and has the signature and address of the debtor, essentially giving notice to all parties of the security interest of the creditor that is filing the financing statement, and giving that claim priority over all other claims that are not perfected or are perfected later, with the possible exception of a PMSI.

A PMSI in *consumer goods*, which is automatically perfected against attachment, having higher priority than all other claims, perfected or not, except a good-faith consumer purchaser of the property; and a higher priority than all claims for property other than inventory, including a good-faith consumer purchaser of the property, if a financing statement is filed within 20 days of attachment.

R191705   **Secured Transactions**   R191706

ROGER CPA Review

REG - TERM

Chapter 7 Bankruptcy

Chapter 11 Bankruptcy

Bankruptcy

ROGER CPA Review

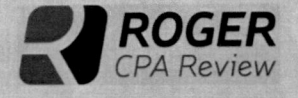

REG - DEFINITION

A form of bankruptcy applicable to businesses and individuals under which the debtor's assets are *liquidated* and the creditors are paid according to the priority of their claims. This may be entered into either voluntarily by the debtor or involuntarily by the creditors.

A form of bankruptcy, also referred to as a *reorganization*, applicable to businesses under which the debtor continues to operate the business and establishes a plan, agreed upon by creditors, as to how obligations will be satisfied.

R201701

Bankruptcy

R201702

REG - TERM

Chapter 13 Bankruptcy

Involuntary Petition

Bankruptcy

ROGER CPA Review

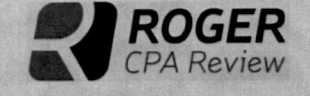

REG - DEFINITION

A form of bankruptcy, also referred to as a *debt adjustment plan*, applicable to individuals and small businesses under which a debtor earning sufficient income proposes a detailed plan for the repayment of debt, generally over 3 to 5 years, subject to the approval of the courts.

A debtor being forced into bankruptcy under either Chapter 7 or Chapter 11 by creditors who are not being paid on a timely basis, requiring the signatures of 3 or more creditors with unsecured claims aggregating at least $15,775 (as of 4/16) when there are 12 or more creditors; and requiring the signature of only one creditor with unsecured claims aggregating that same amount when there are fewer than 12.

Bankruptcy

REG - TERM

Avoiding Powers | Preferential Transfers

Bankruptcy

ROGER CPA Review

REG - DEFINITION

The ability of the trustee in bankruptcy to retrieve property that has been transferred to creditors or other third parties to maximize the assets available to creditors if they result from (**FLAP**):

- **F**raudulent transfers,
- Statutory **L**iens,
- Post-petition transfers (**A**fter the filing), or
- **P**referential transfers of property.

Transfers made by the debtor in anticipation of bankruptcy that resulted in giving a creditor a more favorable settlement than would have been achieved through bankruptcy, characterized as (**I-WAIT**):

- Debtor was **I**nsolvent when the transfer was made;
- Occurring **W**ithin 90 days of the filing of the petition;
- In settlement of an **A**ntecedent debt (preexisting — existed as of the date of the filing);
- **I**mproves the creditor's relative position; and
- **T**ime increased from 90 days to 1 year if the transfer was made to an insider (relative or close relative of debtor).

Bankruptcy

REG - TERM

Nonpreferential Transfers

Priority Claims

Bankruptcy

ROGER CPA Review

REG - DEFINITION

Transfers that are not voidable by the trustee, including (*C-CONAC*):

- Payments to **C**harities;
- **C**onsumer debt that is minimal in amount;
- Bills, such as utilities, that are incurred in the **O**rdinary course of business or with the passage of time;
- Transfers made in exchange for **N**ew value;
- Payments for **A**limony and child support; and
- **C**ontinuing payments on installment obligations.

Claims that will be paid, in order and subject to certain limitations, prior to the claims of remaining unsecured (General) creditors, including (*STOP-IT-D*runk driver):

- **S**upport and alimony payments;
- **T**rustee, attorney and other costs of administering the bankruptcy;
- Claims of creditors **O**wed after the filing of the bankruptcy petition;
- **P**ayroll costs up to certain limits;
- **I**ndividual consumer deposits up to certain limits;
- **T**axes for which the statute of limitations has not expired (3 years); and
- **D**runk driver injury claims.

Bankruptcy

ROGER CPA Review

REG - TERM

Exceptions to Discharge | **Denial of Discharge**

Bankruptcy

ROGER CPA Review

REG - DEFINITION

Debts that are not discharged as a result of bankruptcy and remain obligations of the debtor, including obligations for alimony or child support; credit card purchases of luxury goods, large cash advances, and auto loans; student loans; loans obtained through false representation; debts that were omitted by the debtor when disclosing all obligations; taxes; obligations resulting from violations of securities laws under Sarbanes-Oxley; and drunk driver injury claims.

The debtor not receiving relief and remaining liable for all obligations as a result of inadequate books and records, including the destruction of records; refusal to provide information as to the location of assets; committing a bankruptcy offense, such as withholding records or refusing to obey a court order; having received a discharge within a specified period of time; or a fraudulent transfer.

Bankruptcy

ROGER CPA Review

REG - TERM

Creditor Rights

Debtor & Creditor Relationships (Suretyship)

R211701

ROGER CPA Review

REG - DEFINITION

Alternatives for debtors other than bankruptcy, include:

- Agreeing with creditors to pay a proportionate reduced amount in settlement in a *composition with creditors* agreement.
- Voluntarily transferring assets to creditors in an assignment for the benefit of creditors.
- Being required to surrender assets to a creditor as a result of a writ of attachment.
- A creditor's seizure of the debtor's wages or balances in financial institutions through garnishment.
- Creditors having claims to the debtor's property through liens, which may be consensual, such as mortgages, or nonconsensual, such as mechanics' liens.
- Limiting liability due to losses resulting from the fraudulent use of the debtor's credit cards as a result of the Credit Card Fraud Act.
- Exempting a certain portion of the equity in the debtor's residence by applying the homestead exemption.
- Obtaining protection from inappropriate tactics of debt collectors as a result of the Fair Debt Collection Practices Act.

Debtor & Creditor Relationships (Suretyship)   R211701